Élan 2

WJEC

Self Study Guide

Marian Jones

OXFORD

UNIVERSITY PRESS

OXFORD
UNIVERSITY PRESS

Great Clarendon Street, Oxford OX2 6DP

Oxford University Press is a department of the University of Oxford.
It furthers the University's objective of excellence in research, scholarship,
and education by publishing worldwide in

Oxford   New York
Auckland   Cape Town   Dar es Salaam   Hong Kong   Karachi
Kuala Lumpur   Madrid   Melbourne   Mexico City   Nairobi
New Delhi   Shanghai   Taipei   Toronto

With offices in

Argentina   Austria   Brazil   Chile   Czech Republic   France   Greece
Guatemala   Hungary   Italy   Japan   South Korea   Poland   Portugal
Singapore   Switzerland   Thailand   Turkey   Ukraine   Vietnam

Oxford is a registered trade mark of Oxford University Press
in the UK and in certain other countries

British Library Cataloguing in Publication Data

Data available

ISBN 978 019 915412 8

10 9 8 7 6 5 4 3 2 1

Typeset by PDQ Digital Media Solutions Ltd.
Printed in Great Britain by Ashford Colour Press Ltd.

Acknowledgements

The author and publisher would like to thank Deborah Manning (editor)
and Marie-Thérèse Bougard (language consultant).

Contents

General Exam Tips

Here's a reminder of the topics from the WJEC A2 specification which you need to revise for the examination.

Environmental Issues

Including technology pollution, global warming, transport, energy, nuclear energy, renewable energies, conservation, recycling, sustainability.

Social and Political Issues

Including the role of the media, racism, immigration, social exclusion and integration, terrorism, employment, commerce, globalisation.

Guided Studies

In addition, you have to study two cultural topics from the areas listed below. You can do two topics from the same list (e.g. two books, two films or two regions) or choose two from different lists.

The World of Cinema – The World of Literature – The Regions of France

You will be taking two examinations. **Remember** that your AS grade represents 50% of your A Level.

Unit FN3: Oral

The Speaking Test is worth 20% of the 50% available at A2. The test lasts 15–20 minutes and you have 15–20 minutes to prepare beforehand. You are not allowed to use a dictionary. There are two sections:

Structured Discussion (6 minutes)

Oral Exposé (about 14 minutes)

Unit FN4: Listening, Reading and Writing

This paper is worth 30% of the 50% available at A2 and the time allowed is three hours. There are four sections:

Listening and Responding – Reading and Responding – Translation from French to English – Guided Studies Essay

Pass grades for this examination range from A* and A down to E.

The descriptions of what you need to be able to do are very similar to those at AS Level, **but remember that this is in the context of the more demanding texts and tasks which you will meet at A2.** Two things which are expected are an ability to translate from English into French accurately and an ability to cope with the unpredictable when you are talking to someone. Here's a reminder of the other expectations:

If you pass A Level French with an A grade, it means you can:

- ▶ clearly understand spoken language, including details and opinions.
- ▶ work out what someone is trying to say even if they don't spell it out in detail.
- ▶ clearly understand written texts, understanding both the gist and the details.
- ▶ talk fluently, giving your opinions and justifying them, and using a good range of vocabulary and generally accurate pronunciation.
- ▶ organise your ideas and write them up well in French.
- ▶ write using a wide range of vocabulary and grammatical structures without making many mistakes.

If you pass A Level French with an E grade, it means you:

- ▶ show some understanding of spoken French, even if you have difficulties when the language is complex and miss some of the details.
- ▶ can sometimes work out what someone is trying to say even if they don't give all the details.
- ▶ understand straightforward written texts, although you don't always understand more difficult writing.
- ▶ can talk in French, and convey basic information, perhaps a little hesitantly and relying on material you have learned by heart. There is probably some English influence on your pronunciation.
- ▶ can convey information in writing, perhaps with some difficulty in organising your material and expressing it.
- ▶ use a range of vocabulary and structures, but quite often you make mistakes.

Preparing for the exams

You can see from these lists that when planning your revision there are really six areas you need to practise:

Speaking – Listening – Reading – Writing – Vocabulary – Grammar

There are tips on how to prepare each area overleaf.

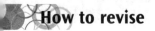

Speaking

▶ Take every opportunity to practise speaking French – in lessons, with the language assistant, with a friend, with anyone you know who speaks French.

▶ To prepare for the Structured Discussion, think up some controversial statements linked to each topic from the first two sections on page 4 and practise arguing for or against them. An example would be *'La prison ne nous aide pas à baisser le taux de criminalité'*. Record your ideas on tape and listen to see what areas still need practice – perhaps fluency, pronunciation or good use of vocabulary and structures.

▶ Keep researching the topic you have chosen for your Oral Exposé, noting both facts and useful vocabulary and expressions. Make notes on your various sub-headings but don't write everything out in full; note just a few key words down for reference, but definitely no full sentences.

Listening

▶ Keep listening to French, ideally every day. Use a mix of extracts you have worked on and new texts.

▶ Try listening to something for which you have the transcript. Just listen first, then listen again with the transcript and, if necessary, look up unknown words. Finally, listen again without the transcript and challenge yourself to understand everything.

▶ Watching films is excellent listening practice and watching more than once is even better! Try watching with the subtitles and then without. If you find this hard going, just re-watch a short extract.

▶ French radio and TV programmes are useful, but can also be difficult. Record an extract and listen or watch it more than once. You will find it gets easier.

▶ Make sure you do some exam listening practice too, using texts with questions in English!

Reading

▶ Keep reading a mix of things you read once quickly, such as a magazine, and things where you work hard at a short passage and try to understand everything. Texts from your textbook are useful for this.

▶ It's useful to note new vocabulary from your reading, but don't make it such hard work that you give up. Note, say, three new words from each text.

▶ Try a 'dual-language' reading book, where you get the original French on one page and an English translation on the opposite one. This is an excellent way to practise reading longer texts without losing heart!

▶ Search on the internet for articles in French on any topic which interests you.

Writing

- ▶ Write out the basic facts for each aspect of the cultural topics you have studied and learn them.
- ▶ Practise planning essay questions on your cultural topics, jotting down ideas for each paragraph – in French! – along with key vocabulary.
- ▶ Look carefully at marked work and identify what grammar errors you are making. Then check them up in a grammar book and try some practice exercises.
- ▶ Make sure you are writing – and learning – lists of key vocabulary for each of the two cultural topics. In addition, learn a good range of 'essay phrases' for introducing ideas, giving opinions, summing up and so on.

Vocabulary

- ▶ Learn lists of words regularly and build in time to go back over words you learned a week or two ago. Reinforcement makes them stick!
- ▶ Choose a system of recording new words which works for you. It could be paper lists, small sections on individual cards, recording the words and their English meanings on tape, making posters to stick on your bedroom wall ... what's important is that you are noting the words and going over them regularly!
- ▶ You were probably encouraged to use a good range of vocabulary in the essays you wrote during the year. Go back over them, highlighting good words and phrases and writing the English in the margin, then use this to test yourself. Words are often easier to learn in context.

Grammar

- ▶ Keep doing practice exercises in areas where you know you are weak.
- ▶ Use reading texts to practise thinking grammatically. For example, highlight a selection of adjectives, then write out the English for the phrases in which they appear. Test yourself by reproducing the French phrases accurately, complete with all the correct agreements.
- ▶ Keep learning from your verb tables until you know all the forms of each tense of regular verbs and the most common irregular verbs. Test yourself using a die. 1 = *je*, 2 = tu, 3 = *il/elle*, 4 = *nous*, 5 = *vous*, 6 = *ils/elles*. Use a verb list, choose an infinitive and a tense at random, throw the die and say the correct form of the verb. Practise until you can do it without hesitation.

Speaking

The Speaking Test: what you need to know

The test has two parts: a structured discussion and an oral exposé and discussion on one of the cultural topics you chose from the Guided Studies list.

Structured Discussion (6 minutes)

You will be given a short text to study during the preparation period of 15–20 minutes and you can make notes on it, but are not allowed the use of a dictionary. The text will usually contain some kind of argument or discussion point.

- ▶ First, you will be asked a few questions about the text.
- ▶ Then, you will be asked to give your own views on the topic and discuss them with the examiner who may challenge them to see if you can defend your argument. During the preparation time it is a good idea to anticipate this and, in addition to preparing your argument, try to predict the arguments the examiner might use and to plan how you will counter them.
- ▶ You will not be allowed to read out your notes verbatim, so it's best to jot down brief reminders, useful vocabulary and expressions for agreeing or disagreeing with someone, but not to try and write out in full sentences exactly what you hope to say.

To do well on this section you need to respond readily and spontaneously to the examiner's arguments, speak fluently without much hesitation and show that you can present a good argument, clearly conveying and justifying your opinions.

Oral Exposé (about 14 minutes)

You have to choose one of the cultural topics you have studied and prepare brief notes on it under 5–10 headings. You present the topic to the examiner for a maximum of four minutes, then discuss it and issues arising from it with him or her.

To do well on this section, you need to know your topic thoroughly, present some interesting arguments and defend them well, as well as showing a good level of fluency.

In addition, both sections of the oral are marked for accuracy and for range of language, which includes both a wide vocabulary and a varied range of grammatical structures. Lastly, marks are awarded for convincing, French-sounding pronunciation.

On vous demande de participer à une discussion au sujet de ce texte avec l'examinateur ou l'examinatrice. Regardez le texte et réfléchissez aux questions suivantes qui serviront de point de départ à la discussion.

Un match pour dire non au racisme

En réaction aux incidents et aux violences, de plus en plus courants dans les tribunes des terrains de football, le Stade-Malherbe a installé, samedi après-midi, un village maghrébin sur l'esplanade du stade d'Ornano.

Au gré des tentes berbères, samedi, les passants ont pu goûter les fameuses pâtisseries marocaines, arrosées de thé vert à la menthe, se faire des tatouages au henné, se balader à dos de chameaux ou essayer des bijoux et des robes de danseuses orientales. Ce n'était pas le souk *, mais on s'y croyait presque.

Qui mieux que SOS Racisme pouvait orchestrer cette journée, placée sous le signe de la tolérance et de la lutte contre le racisme? « Nous partageons des valeurs communes avec le sport: la citoyenneté, l'égalité, le vivre ensemble », explique Corinne Jacquemin, présidente de SOS Racisme Calvados. « Nous sommes les porte-parole des spectateurs qui se sentent traumatisés par ce qui se passe dans les stades. La situation est alarmante et il est urgent d'éradiquer la violence. » Pour sensibiliser les passants à leur message, les membres de l'association ont distribué des autocollants « Carton rouge au racisme » et Dominique Sopo, président de l'association nationale, est venu donner le coup d'envoi du match Caen-Valenciennes.

Pour afficher pleinement les positions du club et de ses supporters, une banderole ** publicitaire portant l'inscription 'Touche pas à mon foot' a été réalisée et présentée par les jeunes du centre de formation avant le match.

* souk – mot arabe pour marché

** banderole – petite bannière

1. De quoi ce texte parle-t-il?
2. Peut-on combattre le racisme en organisant de tels événements?
3. Quel rôle les jeunes ont-ils à jouer à cet égard?

Use this text for practice. Plan your answers to the three questions. Then try to think of ways in which the examiner might challenge your views and plan out what you would say then. There are some ideas on page 10.

Here are some examples of possible exchanges based on the text on page 9. Look at the examples below, where the examiner challenges the candidate and try to think of a good response. Then compare your ideas with those at the bottom of the page.

If you say this:	The examiner might say this:
1 Je ne crois pas que la plupart des amateurs de foot soient racistes.	Vraiment? On lit toujours des articles dans la presse qui racontent des incidents racistes, par exemple des gens qui crient des insultes aux joueurs étrangers.
2 Je trouve que ce type d'événement peut encourager les gens à accepter ceux d'une autre culture.	Vous ne trouvez pas qu'il s'agit plutôt de stéréotypes, les tentes berbères, les balades dos de chameau et tout ça?
3 Je trouve que c'est une excellente idée de distribuer des autocollants avec des slogans anti-racistes.	Je suis de l'opinion que c'est un petit geste qui ne changera pas grand-chose.

Learn some useful phrases for disagreeing with the examiner … politely!

Examples are:

Ah non, je ne suis pas du tout d'accord, parce que …

Oui, peut-être, mais il ne faut pas oublier que …

Au contraire, moi je trouve que …

Oui, mais en revanche n'est-il pas vrai que …?

Here are some possible ways to counter what the examiner said:

1 Je crois que ce sont plutôt des exceptions, et que les journalistes aiment raconter tout cela. Je suis convaincu(e) que la plupart des gens sont tolérants et ont horreur de ces incidents provoqués par quelques individus atypiques.

2 Oui, un peu, mais je pense aussi que ces évènements aident à sensibiliser les gens. Si on n'a pas d'amis arabes, par exemple, on n'apprend rien sur leur culture, et un tel marché vous donne l'occasion d'apprendre à la connaître un petit peu.

3 Au contraire, un autocollant est vu par beaucoup de gens, qui passeront un petit moment à réfléchir. Cela aide à faire circuler des idées positives, à dire qu'il y a plein de gens qui sont contre le racisme.

Here's another example of a text for discussion.

On vous demande de participer à une discussion au sujet de ce texte avec l'examinateur ou l'examinatrice. Regardez le texte et réfléchissez aux questions suivantes qui serviront de point de départ à la discussion.

La Saison culturelle européenne, une première de grande envergure organisée par la France à partir du 1er juillet, constitue une chance exceptionnelle de découvrir la diversité créatrice des 27 états membres. Elle est aussi emblématique de la Présidence française de l'Union Européenne, qui débutera à la même date.

Un programme de plusieurs centaines de manifestations, dans toute l'Europe et dans toutes les disciplines artistiques : 27 livres, 27 spectacles, 27 concerts, 27 expositions, 27 leçons d'histoire, des panoramas thématiques sur le cinéma, la photographie, le théâtre, le design, l'art contemporain, les musiques actuelles, le tout rassemblant les plus grands créateurs actuels, s'annonce ambitieux. Initiée avec une foule de partenaires mais en premier lieu par les ministères de la Culture et des Affaires étrangères, la Saison culturelle européenne, du 1er juillet au 31 décembre, sera le premier acte de la Présidence française de l'Union européenne.

Des « projets tandems » regroupent des artistes de plusieurs nationalités autour d'une œuvre ou d'un thème. Il en est ainsi de la chorégraphie hip-hop franco-allemande *Il était une fois*, du spectacle franco-slovène Course à l'amour, de celui que prépare l'actrice française Juliette Binoche et le chorégraphe Akram Khan, du concert de jazz adaptation de l'œuvre de Maurice Duruflé pour le grand Chœur national de Lettonie ...

Un partenariat a également été noué avec l'Éducation nationale afin de sensibiliser le jeune public européen, ainsi des milliers d'apprentis de tous les pays de l'Union Européenne feront un stage à la Cité de l'architecture.

---

1 De quoi s'agit-il dans ce texte?
2 Cela vaut-il la peine d'organiser une telle saison culturelle?
3 Ici, on utilise la culture pour promouvoir une cause politique. Croyez-vous que ce soit une bonne idée?

> It's always a good idea to try and predict what the examiner could ask on a text. Have another look at this one and think up a few more possible questions, then decide how you would answer them.

Read and listen to the beginning of this student's speaking test (CD track 2). He is discussing the text on page 11.

De quoi s'agit-il dans ce texte?

On parle d'une saison culturelle qu'on va organiser pour fêter la diversité créatrice qui existe dans les 27 pays de l'Union Européenne.

Est-ce que cela est la seule raison?

Je crois que c'est la raison principale, mais on veut aussi faire quelque chose pour marquer le début de la présidence française de l'Union. La saison débutera à la même date, donc je crois que ça doit être une raison aussi.

Qui organise tout cela?

Ce sont surtout deux ministères, le ministère de la Culture et le ministère des Affaires étrangères, mais il y aura beaucoup d'autres organisations qui travailleront en partenariat avec eux.

Qu'est-ce qui se passera pendant la saison culturelle?

Il y aura un énorme choix d'événements, par exemple des spectacles, des concerts et des expositions. Ils auront lieu dans toute l'Europe, pas seulement en France et les artistes des divers pays travailleront ensemble. Par exemple, il y aura 27 concerts, j'imagine que c'est parce qu'il y a 27 membres de l'UE.

Cela vaut-il la peine d'organiser une telle saison culturelle?

Je crois que oui. Beaucoup de gens s'intéressent à la culture.

Oui, peut-être, mais pas tout le monde. Et cela doit coûter cher.

Oui, sans doute. Mais on a vraiment essayé d'organiser quelque chose pour tout le monde. Il y a de tout, et si vraiment il y a des gens qui n'aiment ni la musique, ni la littérature, enfin qui n'aiment pas la culture, voilà une occasion pour apprendre quelque chose!

Ici, on utilise la culture pour promouvoir une cause politique. Croyez-vous que ce soit une bonne idée?

Je ne vois pas pourquoi ce serait un problème. Si on pense que l'Union Européenne est importante, c'est un bon moyen de montrer son importance aux gens. Si on voit des artistes de différents pays qui travaillent ensemble, on se rendra compte que tous ces pays peuvent co-opérer. Cela donne un message positif, je trouve.

Structuring your oral exposé is really important. You need to make it easy for the examiner to follow – remember s/he will be listening to lots of presentations that day and you will do both of you a favour if yours is clear and logical. Use some 'marker' phrases to guide the examiner through what you are saying:

J'ai décidé de faire des recherches sur …
D'abord, je vais vous expliquer …
Je peux aussi citer quelques exemples de …
Ensuite, j'espère vous donner des détails sur …
Et finalement, je voudrais décrire …

Of course research and a good knowledge of your topic are vital. But do not try to pack everything into the exposé. It is better to highlight the main areas you want to cover, perhaps mentioning one or two facts as 'appetisers', inviting the examiner to come back to that aspect and ask you more. For each aspect mentioned in your exposé, you need a set of well-organised notes. Write the key facts for each and learn them: you won't be asked to recite them, but you will be able to slip them in as examples to illustrate the points you are making. Knowing your material really well will give you the confidence to speak fluently.

Remember that the examiner will be interested in your opinions and whether you can justify them. For practice, work out how the following question openings could be used to ask questions on your topic. They are the sort of question you are likely to be asked, so plan how you would answer them.

Que pensez-vous de …
Peut-on justifier …?
Jusqu'à quel point peut-on dire que …
Aimez-vous …?
Pouvez-vous expliquer la popularité de …

Once everything is planned, you just need to practise! Make a note of the questions you are asked in practice sessions with your teacher or the assistant, so that you gradually build up a list of things you can answer well. You can practise on your own by using these questions and recording your responses. Listen to them with the WJEC mark scheme in front of you and analyse how you are doing.

You can listen to ten students answering sample questions from this section on the CD (track 3). You'll find the transcripts in a word document on the CD ROM.

The Listening, Reading and Writing paper

The time allowed for this paper is three hours and you are free to plan your time as you wish.

Question 1: Listening (6 marks)

You listen to a passage of French and answer questions on it in English. You can listen to the passage as many times as you like and pause or rewind it if you wish.

Questions 2a and 2b: Reading (22 marks = 12 + 10)

You read two passages in French and answer questions on them in French.

Question 3: Translation (25 marks)

You are asked to translate an English passage of about 100 words into French.

Question 4: Writing (45 marks)

You have to write an essay of about 400 words on one topic from either *The World of Cinema* or *The World of Literature* or *The Regions of France*. There is a choice of two questions on every topic on the list of Guided Studies, i.e. 18 questions altogether on films, 18 on books and 18 on regions.

The key ways to prepare are by:

► doing plenty of listening practice to keep your ear 'tuned in' to French

► reading a wide variety of materials linked to the topics listed on page 4

► working through English passages to translate into French, keeping a careful note of new vocabulary and checking up on grammar points on which you are making errors

► practising writing 400 word essays on the cultural topics you have studied

► working through the exam-type questions and tips on the following pages.

Vengeance   CD track 4

Listen to the report, then answer the following questions in English.

a What happened in L'Haÿ-Les-Roses this weekend?
b What developments have there been since Sunday?
c Describe the two attempts at the crime.
d What did a witness see?
e What did the police want to clarify during the custody period?
f What extra detail do we learn about the victims at the end of the report?

> Be especially careful over questions needing several bits of information and be sure you give all the relevant detail. When you have done this exercise, read the answer section carefully and take note of all the details required for questions **a**, **b** and **c**.

a There was a fire in a block of flats and 18 people were killed.
b Four girls aged 15–18 have been remanded in custody.
c At first, they tried to set fire to the letterbox, but this didn't work, so they stuffed it with paper and then the fire caught rapidly.
d S/he saw the girls running away.
e Exactly what role each played.
f That three of them were children.

C'est une histoire de 'vengeance' qui a conduit à la mort de 18 personnes dans l'incendie d'un immeuble à L'Haÿ-Les-Roses, dans le Val-de-Marne, ce week-end. Les quatre jeunes filles, âgées de 15 à 18 ans, placées en garde à vue depuis dimanche à Paris, ont avoué les faits.

'L'histoire de vengeance' visait une autre jeune fille de la cité, Nadia. Les quatre suspects âgées de 15 à 18 ans visaient la boîte aux lettres de Nadia. Deux d'entre elles ont tenté de mettre le feu une première fois à la boîte samedi soir et ont échoué. Elles ont alors décidé de placer des papiers en vrac dans et autour de la boîte. Cette fois, le feu a pris rapidement. Les jeunes filles ont alors pris la fuite, dépassées par les évènements, mais un voisin les a vues et a appelé la police. Les jeunes filles sont passées aux aveux dimanche soir et ont été interpellées dans la nuit de dimanche à lundi puis lundi matin. Le rôle précis de chacune restait à affiner dans le cours de la garde à vue. Deux sont soupçonnées d'avoir mis le feu, les deux autres faisant le guet. Elles ont été présentées toutes les quatre à la justice mardi. L'incendie a tué au total 18 personnes, dont trois enfants, selon le dernier bilan.

Contre le racisme

Lisez le texte, puis répondez en français aux questions ci-dessous.

Elles étaient toutes là. SOS racisme, la Ligue contre le racisme et l'antisémitisme (Licra), la ligue des droits de l'homme (LDH), l'union des étudiants juifs de France (UEJF).

Les associations qui luttent contre les discriminations ont appelé hier à un rassemblement citoyen au pub My Goodness, dont le gérant avait déposé plainte contre cinq hommes qui avaient tenu des propos antisémites et racistes dans son établissement dans la nuit du 1er au 2 février dernier. Une bonne raison pour tous les candidats potentiels aux élections municipales ou cantonales de faire le déplacement.

Maître Hubert Delarue, l'avocat du gérant, et maire-adjoint de la ville, avait deux casquettes: « Mon client a été surpris et choqué par le comportement des cinq individus dont trois font encore partie de la police nationale. Il ne souhaite pas qu'il y ait un amalgame entre le comportement de ces trois policiers et la police nationale. Cet homme veut panser ses plaies et retrouver le plus rapidement possible l'anonymat dans lequel il se trouvait avant l'affaire », dit l'avocat.

1 Quel est le lien entre les quatre organisations mentionnées dans le premier paragraphe?
2 Décrivez l'incident qui s'est passé dans le pub My Goodness.
3 Que voulaient montrer les candidats aux élections municipales en venant au rassemblement?
4 Qu'est-ce qui est surprenant concernant trois des cinq individus accusés?
5 Que veut faire la victime maintenant?

You can often use ideas and short phrases from the text, but you should not be copying whole sentences from it and will usually have to adapt the language. For question 2, the part about the five men who caused trouble in the pub is expressed using the pluperfect tense, because the text recounts how the landlord phoned the police about the men who **had** caused trouble. You will need to adapt the wording and use the perfect tense for your answer. For question 5, try to think of synonyms for the expressions 'panser ses plaies' and 'retrouver l'anonymat', or at least to re-word the expressions. See the answers for suggestions.

5 Il veut se remettre et redevenir anonyme.

4 Trois d'entre eux font partie de la police nationale.

3 Ils voulaient montrer qu'ils sont contre le racisme.

2 Cinq hommes ont tenu des propos racistes dans le pub My Goodness.

1 Elles luttent toutes contre le racisme ou la discrimination.

Aide et Action

Lisez le texte 'Aide et Action', puis répondez aux questions suivantes en français.

Voulez-vous parrainer un enfant du tiers-monde? Contactez-nous! Le parrainage Aide et Action vous permettra d'établir une relation personnalisée avec un enfant pendant l'ensemble de sa scolarisation de 6 à 8 ans.

Pour toute cette durée, vous vous engagez à soutenir financièrement Aide et Action dans ses démarches pour une éducation au service du développement, dans tous les pays où elle intervient, à hauteur de 20€ minimum par mois.

En 2004, il y avait 60 000 parrains et donateurs, mais l'argent que vous donnez nous permet de soutenir plus de 2 millions d'enfants en tout, parce que ce sont les écoles qui reçoivent les fonds et non pas les individus. Cependant, les enfants parrainés jouent un rôle essentiel, ils sont les "ambassadeurs" de leur école vis-à-vis des parrains et des marraines.

Lors de la réception de votre demande, nous vous envoyons un dossier avec l'histoire personnelle de l'enfant et sa photo. Vous recevrez trois correspondances par an et deux photos durant le parrainage.

a Quelles personnes sont priées de contacter Aide et Action?
b Qu'est-ce que le parrainage offre aux donateurs?
c Le parrainage dure combien de temps?
d Le soutien financier des parrains s'élève à combien?
e Expliquez comment les parrains soutiennent la communauté entière.
f Que recevront les parrains au début du parrainage?

> Being able to manipulate the verbs in the text is a useful skill. The suggested answer for question **a** adapts *voulez-vous* from the text into *Ceux qui veulent* to begin the answer. Sometimes you can use the verb form from the question, as in question **f** where the suggested answer begins *Ils recevront …*

f Ils recevront un dossier avec l'histoire personnelle de l'enfant et sa photo.

e L'argent qu'ils donnent soutient une école et non pas un enfant en particulier.

d Ils doivent contribuer un minimum de 20 euros par mois.

c Il dure environ 6 ou 8 ans.

b On leur offre l'occasion d'établir une relation personnalisée avec un enfant du tiers-monde et de soutenir sa scolarisation.

a Ceux qui veulent parrainer un enfant du tiers-monde sont priés de contacter Aide et Action.

In the exam you have to translate a passage of about 100 words into French, but translating individual sentences is good practice too.

Traduisez en français les phrases suivantes:

a Nowadays petrol is becoming more and more expensive.
b We should encourage people to leave their car at home.
c Fast cars are fun but they waste a lot of energy.
d We could also do something for the environment by not flying very often.
e If your ideal holiday is at the beach, find a beach near you!
f But although we understand the problem, we do not want to do these things.
g No-one knows what will happen in the future.

Think grammatically! Which sentence or sentences require you to use each of the following? Work it out, then check the answers below.

  i the construction *en* + present participle
 ii a verb which is followed by *à*
iii a phrase followed by the subjunctive
 iv an adjective which will need agreement
  v a negative construction which isn't *ne … pas*
 vi a comparative
vii a verb in the conditional tense
viii a verb in the future tense
 ix *ce qui* or *ce que* (which do you need here?)

i d ii b iii f iv c and e v g vi a vii b and d viii g ix ce qui

Remember that you can't always translate word for word. The best translation for 'nowadays' is not a single word, but a phrase and 'near you' is best translated by four words, not two.

Check everything very carefully. Is every verb in the correct tense and does it agree with its subject? Does every adjective which needs agreement have it?

a De nos jours, l'essence devient de plus en plus chère.
b Nous devrions encourager les gens à laisser leur voiture chez eux.
c Les voitures rapides sont amusantes, mais elles gaspillent beaucoup d'énergie.
d Nous pourrions aussi faire quelque chose pour l'environnement en ne prenant pas l'avion trop souvent.
e Si vos vacances idéales sont à la plage, cherchez une plage près de chez vous!
p Mais bien que nous comprenions le problème, nous ne voulions pas faire ces choses.
e Personne ne sait ce qui se passera dans l'avenir.

Translate into French.

We must all try not to waste the earth's resources. Everyone can make small gestures, such as switching lights off when leaving a room or turning down the central heating. But is that enough?

Young people need to accept that we will no longer be able to drive everywhere as we used to. Anyone who has bought a car should leave it in the garage as often as possible. Car-sharing is one solution and allows you to save money and to pollute the atmosphere less.

Most people could do better. We know it's irresponsible to buy goods with lots of packaging or to live on ready meals. We ought to make a little more effort.

Always try to spot the 'grammar tricks' the examiner has planted in the English passage. To translate the first paragraph well, you need to remember that *ne* and *pas* come together before an infinitive and that you can use the infinitive of a French verb to translate the English present participle forms 'switching off' and 'turning down'. But to translate 'leaving' in this context, you need *en* + a present participle.

Be especially careful over the spelling of words which are similar to, but not quite the same as, their English equivalents. In this passage, words like this include the translations of 'resources', 'polluting', 'atmosphere' and 'irresponsible'.

When checking your translation, look especially at the verb forms. Have you got the right parts of *devoir* to translate 'We must all …' in the first paragraph and 'Young people need to …' in the second? Have you correctly translated the future and perfect tenses needed in the second paragraph?

Suggested translation

Nous devons tous essayer de ne pas gaspiller les ressources de la terre. Tout le monde peut faire des petits gestes, comme éteindre les lumières en sortant d'une pièce ou baisser le chauffage central. Mais est-ce que cela suffit?

Les jeunes doivent accepter que nous ne pourrons plus conduire partout, comme on le faisait autrefois. Celui ou celle qui a acheté une voiture devrait la laisser au garage le plus souvent possible. Le co-voiturage est une solution et permet de faire des économies et de moins polluer l'atmosphère.

La plupart des gens pourraient faire mieux. Nous savons qu'il est irresponsable d'acheter des marchandises avec beaucoup d'emballages ou de vivre de plats préparés. Il faudrait faire un plus gros effort.

The Essay Question

What kind of question will you be asked? Here are some typical areas likely to be covered. Make sure you are prepared for a question on any of them.

The World of Cinema / The World of Literature

Development and plot
Relationships
The personalities of the main characters
Individual viewpoints and beliefs
Motivation for actions
(Also, for cinema, how cinematic devices relate to these aspects, e.g. sound, colour, flashbacks, slow motion, etc. You will not, however, be asked to write a detailed essay on cinema technology or production methods.)

The Regions of France

Geography
Economic factors
Recent history
Society
Culture, traditions and lifestyle

How is the essay marked?

There are 45 marks in total, given as follows:

Quality of Response: 15 marks, i.e. a well-planned, logical answer which is totally relevant to the question. You need to show an ability to analyse and evaluate and to back up your argument with factual information.

Knowledge of Topic and Text: 10 marks, i.e. you need to show wide knowledge of the topic which is relevant to the question and to be able to draw on it to support your arguments.

Accuracy: 10 marks, i.e. you must be able to explain your arguments in mainly accurate French, for example using verb tenses and adjectival agreements correctly and writing even complex sentences with only occasional errors.

Range and Idiom: 10 marks, i.e. you show a wide vocabulary and a good knowledge of grammatical structures. You write idiomatically, in a good essay style.

Writing an Essay on a Cultural Topic

You have to write one essay of about 450 words on one of the cultural topics you have studied. The three vital stages are planning, writing and checking.

Planning

Don't rush this stage. 5–10 minutes thinking about the question, deciding on your argument and dividing it into paragraphs, jotting down the facts you want to use and thinking out a good introduction and conclusion is time very well spent. Keep referring to the title to make sure every paragraph is relevant to the question. You might also note vocabulary and phrases you want to use in each paragraph. Then, when everything is in order, start writing, and make sure you stick to the plan!

Writing

Work through your notes for each paragraph. Write them up using a variety of sentence lengths, interesting vocabulary and a range of grammatical constructions. Be especially careful about the links between the paragraphs, so the examiner can follow the argument easily. See the ideas on page 23.

Checking

Read your essay once through to check the flow of ideas and make sure each sentence makes sense. Then do a more detailed check, looking especially for these common errors:

- ▶ verbs which don't agree with their subject or are in the wrong tense
- ▶ adjectives which don't match the noun they describe
- ▶ phrases which are not idiomatic and don't sound French
- ▶ misspellings, especially of words similar to, but not the same as, English
- ▶ missing accents.

It's also useful to practise planning essays, even if you don't write them up in full. Writing well-thought-out plans for possible essay titles is excellent revision in itself, and gives you some materials to look over in the last revision periods before the exam.

Make some useful revision notes by copying out sentences from your essays which had mistakes in them and then putting in the corrections in a different colour. Doing this will remind you of errors you have made and – even more importantly – remind you how to correct them!

Structuring your essay

Obviously, your essay needs a beginning, a middle and an end, but there are different ways to plan it. Here are a few possibilities:

► For and against
This is the classic 'balanced argument' technique where you write one or two paragraphs in favour of something, then one or two more against it and then conclude with your personal opinion.

► Tennis match
This is another useful way to structure an essay in which you want to put forward both sides of an argument. Each paragraph is used to put forward a point from one side of the argument, then give the reasons against it. It is useful if you want to put one side of the argument over strongly; each paragraph gives a reason for your argument, then explains why those opposed to it are wrong. The essay then needs to end with a strong conclusion.

► Chronological
A chronological approach is suitable for certain types of question. An essay about plot development in a film or a novel can follow this pattern, as long as you careful not to lapse into just re-telling the story. You may want to describe a character at the beginning of the story, refer to events which happen and the effect it has on him or her and then conclude by saying how he or she has changed. It could also be a useful aproach for an essay on, say, the impact of tourism in a particular region, if you wanted to explain how the industry has developed over time.

► Build the argument
Some essays practically plan themselves! If you want to write about the way cinematic techniques contribute to plot development in a film, you may decide that the relevant points are sound, lighting, the use of flashbacks and the range of camera angles used. So it makes sense to devote one paragraph to each of those, making each point clear by giving examples and then saying what the effect of each is. Top and tail this with an introduction and conclusion (see page 23) and you have a perfect plan.

> Make a point of using different styles of essay plan in the practice essays you write so you become familiar with the possibilities and see what works best in each particular set of circumstances.

The essay: making your points

▶ The beginning

Your introduction needs to set the scene. It should pose the question you will be answering, but not give away your conclusion. Look at these notes for possible introductions for particular titles.

Analysez les sentiments anti-sémitiques dans le film *Au revoir les enfants*.

L'action du film *Au revoir les enfants* se déroule pendant la deuxième guerre mondiale, une période de fort anti-sémitisme. Je vais expliquer ce qu'on apprend sur ce fléau dans le film et analyser le comportement de certains gens de l'époque qui nous semble parfois incompréhensible.

'Sans la pêche, la Bretagne serait une région sous-développée.' Analysez et commentez cette idée.

Les cartes postales bretonnes montrent souvent des bateaux de pêche dans un petit port pittoresque, mais est-ce vrai que la Bretagne dépend exclusivement de cette industrie? Je vais expliquer l'importance de la pêche pour la région, mais aussi analyser la contribution à l'économie bretonne d'autres sources de revenu comme le tourisme, le nucléaire et les nouvelles technologies. Je pourrai alors répondre à la question 'Où en serait la Bretagne sans la pêche?'.

▶ The middle

Stick to the paragraph plan you have worked out. Make it easy for the examiner to follow your argument by 'signposting' it, giving an idea at the beginning of each new paragraph what point you are going to make and how it follows on from the previous paragraph. Is it another point in the same argument or does it contradict your previous point?

Adding a new argument:
Il faut aussi constater que ...
En plus, je dois dire que ...
N'oublions pas non plus que ...
Il en est de même pour ...
En outre ...

Contradicting your previous point:
En revanche ...
Au contraire ...
Mais tout le monde n'est pas d'accord. Certains pensent que ...
Cependant, ce n'est pas toujours le cas. Par exemple, ...
Est-ce vrai? Pas forcément. Citons par exemple ...

▶ The end

The conclusion is the place to answer the question and to give your personal viewpoint, which should arise logically out of the arguments you have put forward, Useful phrases include:

J'en conclus donc que ...
Toute réflexion faite, je trouve que ...
Après avoir pesé le pour et le contre, je pense que ...
En fin de compte, je crois que ...

All the grammar you learned for AS is still needed and there are some extra points for A2. Pages 25–30 revise AS grammar, reminding you what you should know and giving you phrases and sentences to translate from and into French for practice. Pages 31–33 revise the points you will be learning on the A2 course, which are also practised through sentences to translate.

Grammar is even more important at A2 than it was at AS. So, what can you do to make sure you really do know your stuff?

Pay attention when grammar is explained! If you learn the rules and the exceptions and do some practice exercises, you will be surprised how much of it will stick.

Accept that there is quite a lot of detail to master and be prepared to go over things regularly. Re-read your grammar notes, re-do practice exercises, and ask questions if you come across things you don't fully understand.

Be pro-active. Go through marked written work, looking carefully at the things which have been corrected. Decide which ones are 'silly mistakes', caused by forgetting things which you know well, and make a list of them, so you can try to avoid them in the future. Then look for errors where you are not quite sure why it is wrong. Ask, if necessary, then look that grammar point up in the grammar section of your textbook and in the relevant section of the grammar workbook. Keep practising and asking questions until you do understand it. When you understand it, review it by writing grammar notes on it in your own words, adding examples.

Make a list of example sentences from your written work which use some of the more complex grammar points well. Learn them, and use them as models for other sentences with different vocabulary but which use the same basic structure. Make a point of including a good variety of grammatical structures in the practice essays you write.

Work through the exercises on the following pages. If there are practice sentences you find hard to translate, learn the correct version from the answer section by heart.

Revision of AS Grammar: nouns, adjectives, adverbs

Check the grammar section of *Élan 2* and/or the Grammar Workbook if you need to know more about any of these things:

▶ typical masculine endings for nouns, such as *-é, -eur, -ment, -age, -isme, -eau*, etc

▶ typical feminine endings for nouns, such as *-ée, -ère, -euse, -itude, -té, -tion*, etc

▶ nouns ending in *-s, -x* or *-z* usually stay the same in the plural and nouns like '*animal*' and '*jeu*' form their plural using *x*

▶ how to use *du, de la, de l'* and *des* to mean 'some' or 'any' and to use *de* in the negative

▶ how to make regular adjectives agree by adding *-e, -s* or *-es*

▶ how to use irregular adjectives like *beau, nouveau, long, bon, frais, gros* and *vieux*

▶ forming possessive adjectives like *mon, ma, mes, notre, votre, nos,* etc

▶ forming adverbs using the feminine form of the adjective plus *-ment* and irregular adverbs like *constamment* and *énormément*

▶ using *plus, moins* and *aussi* to form comparisons and *le plus* or *le moins* to form superlatives

▶ using irregular comparisons like *meilleur* and *pire* or irregular superlatives like *le mieux* and *le pire*.

(1) Translate into English:

1 Il faut utiliser de l'eau moins chaude dans la machine à laver.
2 On voit une exploitation forestière peu respectueuse de la nature.
3 On attend mieux la prochaine fois!
4 Les gaz carboniques ont le pire effet sur notre atmosphère.
5 Nous n'avons plus de solutions réalistes.
6 Que faut-il faire pour prendre la bonne voie?
7 Les transports de l'avenir seront beaucoup plus efficaces.
8 Un régime varié est meilleur pour la santé.
9 Je suis nettement plus optimiste que vous.
10 Le soleil nous apporte directement lumière et chaleur.

Translate into French:

11 Trains are less polluting than cars.
12 We have gas, but no petrol.
13 An old car is not good for the environment.
14 A new car is as bad as an old one.
15 Their house has solar panels.
16 My central heating is expensive.
17 There's a good atmosphere in the eco-village.
18 Life there is cheaper than here.
19 Do you recycle newspapers and bottles?
20 Which energy is the cheapest?

9503)

Grammar

Revision of AS Grammar: pronouns

Check the grammar section of *Élan 2* and/or the Grammar Workbook if you need to know more about any of these things:

- ► direct object pronouns: *me, te, le/la, vous, nous, les*
- ► indirect object pronouns: *me, te, lui, nous, vous, leur*
- ► emphatic pronouns, used for emphasis or after prepositions: *moi, toi, lui, elle, nous, vous, eux, elles*
- ► reflexive pronouns used with reflexive verbs: *me, te, se, nous, vous, se*
- ► the pronouns *y* (which replaces *à*) and *en* (which replaces *de*)
- ► the position of pronouns in a sentence, especially when there is more than one: *envoyez-la moi; je ne le lui ai pas donné*
- ► the relative pronouns *qui, que, où* and *dont*.

(2) Translate into English:

1 Les immigrés? Est-ce qu'on leur paie des allocations familiales?
2 Les dernières lois sur l'immigration, tu les connais?
3 Les familles des immigrés se sont installés dans les banlieues.
4 La xénophonie: qui en sont les victimes?
5 On a tous le droit d'avoir la nationalité du pays où on est né.
6 Les immigrés sont venus travailler dans notre pays. Est-ce qu'ils y sont heureux?
7 Nous sommes contre les mesures qui ne respectent pas les droits de l'homme.
8 La France, c'est le pays où j'ai grandi et dont j'ai complètement absorbé la culture.
9 On ne me laisse pas oublier mes racines arabes.
10 Le respect? On ne le leur donne pas toujours.

Translate into French:

11 Explain racism to me.
12 I told them I do not understand it.
13 He lives in Senegal and is very happy there.
14 It is a country which I don't know.
15 Tahiti is a country whose climate is very nice.
16 They are Polynesians who live in France.
17 They have lived there for 20 years.
18 The map? Show me it, please.
19 Xenophobia – what is the cause?
20 We must try to replace it with tolerance.

Revision of AS Grammar: infinitives and the present tense

Check the grammar section of *Élan 2* and/or the Grammar Workbook if you need to know more about any of these things:

- ▶ the use of the infinitive as a noun or in a set of instructions, e.g. *réviser, c'est ennuyeux*
- ▶ the use of the infinitive as the second verb in a clause, e.g. *je n'aime pas **voir** la pauvreté* or *les touristes préfèrent souvent **voyager** dans les pays riches*
- ▶ the infinitive as used after verbs followed by the prepositions *à* and *de*, such as *aider à, essayer de, permettre à quelqu'un de*
- ▶ the present tense of regular verbs in the *-er, -ir* and *-re* groups, such as *regarder, finir, attendre*
- ▶ the present tense of the modal verbs *vouloir, devoir* and *pouvoir*
- ▶ the present tense of irregular verbs, such as *aller, avoir, être, faire, mettre, prendre, venir, dire, lire, écrire* and many less common ones.
- ▶ the use of the present tense with *depuis*
- ▶ the passive form of the present tense in sentences like *les frais sont payés par les ONG.*

(3) **Translate into English:**

1 Tu préfères organiser une campagne ou travailler comme bénévole?
2 Avec leurs bénéfices ils soutiennent des projets communautaires.
3 Recevoir des prix équitables permet aux producteurs de soutenir leur famille.
4 Il faut agir pour créer des conditions plus justes.
5 Depuis une dizaine d'années, le micro-crédit se développe aussi dans les pays du Nord.
6 Nous comptons sur la bonne volonté de tous ceux qui vivent dans des nations en paix.
7 On essaie d'aider ces enfants à retrouver leur joie de vivre.
8 Les images qui sont transmises du tiers-monde sont souvent horrifiantes.
9 Nous devons faire tout ce que nous pouvons pour aider les victimes du tremblement de terre.
10 Pensez à leurs problèmes avant de les juger.

Translate into French:

11 This guarantees a certain standard of living.
12 Do you work for a charity?
13 I want to help people to live an independent life.
14 You can't count on people's goodwill!
15 I hope to be able to help.
16 What have you decided to do?
17 He has been organising campaigns for years.
18 They are doing all they can to build a house.
19 Spending all your money, that's ridiculous!
20 What do people do if they can't find a job?

Revision of AS Grammar: past tenses

Check the grammar section of *Élan 2* and/or the Grammar Workbook if you need to know more about any of these things:

- ▶ the perfect tense with *avoir: j'ai regardé, nous avons décidé, ils ont parlé*
- ▶ the perfect tense with *être: je suis allé(e), elles sont venues, vous êtes parti(s/e/es)*
- ▶ the perfect tense of irregular verbs: *j'ai voulu, il est devenu, nous avons fait*
- ▶ the perfect tense of reflexive verbs: *je me suis levé(e), la situation s'est aggravée*
- ▶ the imperfect tense: *il y avait, on faisait, nous allions*
- ▶ when to use the perfect and imperfect tenses: *j'ai acheté des produits équitables parce que je voulais faire quelque chose pour aider les producteurs dans le tiers-monde*
- ▶ the pluperfect tense: *j'avais vu, j'étais parti(e), nous avions acheté*
- ▶ the perfect participle: *ayant fait, étant venu.*

(4) Translate into English:

1 Le poète Charles Baudelaire a été condamné pour immoralité.
2 En 1919 on a proposé l'expression *Le septième art* pour désigner l'art cinématographique.
3 C'était une époque où la société était dominée par les hommes.
4 Dès qu'il a quitté l'école, François Truffaut a fondé un ciné-club.
5 Pour Camus, dieu n'existait pas, donc il fallait profiter au maximum de sa vie.
6 Godard, Truffaut et Chabrol se sont mis à tourner des films différents.
7 Truffaut a toujours voulu s'inspirer de sa propre vie.
8 Dans *Les quatre cent coups,* le jeune acteur s'est adressé directement à la caméra.
9 Yasmina Reza a grandi dans un milieu culturel. Elle espérait devenir sociologue.
10 Ayant suivi des études de théâtre Yasmina Reza a commencé à travailler comme actrice.

Translate into French:

11 How many people visited the Musée d'Orsay in 2007?
12 This painting was sold for $78,000,000 last year.
13 Albert Camus became a journalist in 1938.
14 In his novels, he always described ordinary people and situations.
15 Berthe Morisot was shocked by the 1874 exhibition.
16 Truffaut always wanted to make realist films.
17 He won a César and an Oscar.
18 Has Yasmina Reza written any poetry?
19 Having been an actress, she began to write plays.
20 Before yesterday, I hadn't seen any of her plays.

Revision of AS Grammar: future and conditional

Check the grammar section of *Élan 2* and/or the Grammar Workbook if you need to know more about any of these things:

▶ using the present tense to refer to things which are going to happen soon, especially if a future time is mentioned: *je vais au ciné ce soir, on regarde le film vendredi prochain*

▶ using *aller* + infinitive to say what is going to happen in the near future: *je vais retourner en bus, nous allons te rendre visite ce week-end*

▶ using *je voudrais, j'aimerais, je pense*, etc + an infinitive to refer to future plans which are not certain: *un jour, je voudrais visiter les États-Unis, tu penses peut-être étudier les maths?*

▶ forming the future tense of regular verbs using the endings *-ai, -as, -a, -ons, -ez, -ont: je travaillerai, il achètera, vous finirez, ils vendront*

▶ forming the future tense of irregular verbs: *j'irai, on fera, elles deviendront*

▶ using the future tense in *si* clauses: *si j'ai mon bac, j'irai à l'université*

▶ using the future tense where English uses the present after *quand: quand il aura de l'argent, il pourra acheter la voiture*

▶ forming the conditional tense using the future stem and imperfect endings *-ais, -ais, -ait, -ions, -iez, -aient* and using it to refer to what 'would' happen: *j'aimerais voir Paris au printemps.*

(5) **Translate into English:**

1 Nous vivrons demain dans un monde piloté par des ordinateurs.
2 Dans l'avenir, des ordinateurs vous aideront à tout choisir.
3 Il ne sera presque plus nécessaire de sortir de la maison.
4 Les décisions des scientifiques auront des conséquences graves.
5 On aura la possibilité de guérir beaucoup de maladies héréditaires.
6 Mais, il n'y aura pas de remède miracle d'ici cinq ans.
7 Toute pollution génétique serait irréversible.
8 Les manipulations génétiques pourraient créer un monde peuplé de personnes trop parfaites.
9 Toute viande devrait porter une étiquette qui indique sa provenance.
10 Si tu me demandais mon opinion, je ne saurais pas quoi dire.

Translate into French:

11 How will we live in the future?
12 There will be computers everywhere.
13 We will do our shopping in the cybermarket.
14 You'll be able to spend your holiday on another planet.
15 What will daily life be like?
16 My computer will help me make decisions.
17 Scientists will have to be very responsible.
18 I would not like to live in a perfect world.
19 People should know more about technology.
20 When you are old you will need computers.

Revision of AS Grammar: negatives

Check the grammar section of *Élan 2* and/or the Grammar Workbook if you need to know more about any of these things:

▶ using *ne* and *pas* to negate a verb, in simple tenses like the present, future, conditional and imperfect: *je n'aime pas, il n'ira pas, nous ne voudrions pas, elles n'avaient pas*

▶ using *ne* and *pas* in more complex tenses like the perfect, pluperfect, future perfect and conditional perfect: *je n'ai pas vu, tu n'avais pas décidé, vous n'aurez pas choisi, ils n'auraient pas acheté*

▶ using negatives in two verb constructions: *tu ne veux pas y aller, nous n'aimons pas voir*

▶ using the other negative expressions: *ne ... jamais, ne ... plus, ne ... que, ne ...que, ne ... rien, ne ... aucun, ne ... ni ... ni*

▶ using *de* in negative constructions involving a noun: *tu n'as pas de stylo? Moi, je n'ai plus d'argent*

▶ using *ne* and *pas* together before an infinitive: *il serait mieux de ne rien dire, je préfère ne pas y aller.*

6 Translate into English:

1 N'oublions pas l'importance de la diversité culturelle.
2 N'ayez pas peur de l'Union Européenne!
3 Pour le moment, l'UE n'a ni président ni armée.
4 Il n'a jamais été question de dire non.
5 Même ceux qui craignent de perdre leur identité ne peuvent pas nier les avantages de l'UE.
6 Nous ne citerons ici que quelques projets comme Airbus et la fusée Ariane.
7 L'UE ne manque pas non plus d'idées pour l'avenir.
8 Ceci est vrai surtout chez les personnes n'ayant pas la nationalité française.
9 Les Irlandais n'auraient-ils pas dû dire 'oui' au traité de Lisbonne?
10 Peut-être préfèrent-ils ne plus être membre de l'UE.

Translate into French:
11 Isn't Poland a member of the EU?
12 He had not voted.
13 You will never visit Russia.
14 The EU has only 27 member states.
15 I would not like to be the EU President!
16 I no longer have a passport.
17 Nothing is more certain.
18 I have not a single euro left.
19 Do you prefer not to take your holidays in Europe?
20 I have neither the time nor the money.

A2 Grammar: the subjunctive

Use the subjunctive:
- ► after verbs expressing doubt in a negative or interrogative form: *je ne pense pas que ..., il n'est pas sûr que ...*
- ► after verbs expressing an emotion or desire: *je suis contente que ..., nous voudrions que ...*
- ► after impersonal verbs such as *il faut que ...*
- ► after certain expressions including *avant que, bien que, afin que, pour que, à condition que ...*
- ► after a relative pronoun when it follows a superlative or negative: *c'est la plus jolie région que je connaisse; je n'ai rien qui puisse t'aider*
- ► after *que* at the beginning of a sentence: *qu'elle revienne ou non!*
- ► after *qui que, quel que, quoi que, où que: qui que ce soit, je ne suis pas là; quoi que je fasse, ils me critiquent.*

To form the present subjunctive, take the *ils* form of the present tense, leave off the final *-ent* and add the endings *-e, -es, -e, -ions, -iez, -ent.* Learn the common irregular forms such as *que j'aille (aller), que j'aie (avoir), que je sois (être), que je fasse (faire), que je puisse (pouvoir).*

The perfect subjunctive is formed quite logically: *pourvu qu'il ne **soit** pas venu; je ne crois pas qu'elle **ait** vu ce qui s'est passé.*

You do not need to form the imperfect subjunctive, but it is used in formal written French, so you need to be able to recognise it: *bien qu'elles ne **fussent** pas riches; avant qu'il **eût** cette maladie.*

(7) **Translate into English:**

1 Nous avons déménagé afin que je puisse aller dans un bon lycée.
2 Pourvu que je sois reçu au bac, je ferai des études universitaires.
3 Bien qu'ils ne soient pas bien rémunérés, ils aiment leur travail.
4 Quoi que tu fasses en France, il faut savoir parler français.
5 Je doute qu'on puisse changer les choses rapidement.
6 Je veux m'intégrer en France, mais je ne pense pas qu'il faille oublier mes origines.
7 Ce n'est pas certain que je sois bien « intégré ».
8 Je ne veux pas que le Front National puisse arriver au pouvoir.
9 Je ne regrette pas que mes parents m'aient toujours parlé en arabe.
10 Ali a honte que sa mère n'ait pas appris à parler le français.

Translate into French:

11 I will go on condition that you come with me.
12 I am pleased that she is far away.
13 He has moved to Paris so that his children can learn French.
14 It is not certain that she is right.
15 We must go and see.
16 We'll have to do some research before you choose a university.
17 It will be good, providing the weather is nice.
18 That is the biggest ice cream I have ever seen.
19 I want to leave before he comes back.
20 Whether he is rich or not, I like him.

A2 Grammar: more about pronouns

You learned a lot about pronouns at AS Level – see page 26 for a reminder – but now you also need to be confident about some less common pronouns.

- ▶ *lequel/laquelle/lesquels/lesquelles* mean 'which' and are used to mean 'which one?' They are also used in mid-sentence after a preposition. *Tu aimes cette maison? Laquelle? C'est le prof avec lequel je me sens le plus à l'aise.*

- ▶ *auquel* means 'to which'. *C'est un sujet auquel je m'intéresse énormément.*

- ▶ *dont* means 'of which'. *C'est un livre intéressant dont j'ai oublié le titre.* It is used to replace *de* in expressions like *avoir besoin de: Voilà le dictionnaire dont j'ai besoin.*

- ▶ the possessive pronouns are *le mien, le tien, le sien, le nôtre, le vôtre, le leur.*

- ▶ the demonstrative pronouns *celui/celle/ceux/celles* mean 'the one which'. *Tu as vu quel film? Celui avec Jean Reno. Vous voyez cet homme-là? Lequel? Celui à la longue barbe grise.*

(8) Translate into English:

1 Les belles filles? Lesquelles?
2 Et les billets de cent euros. Ce sont les vôtres?
3 C'est un homme auquel je dois tout.
4 Je vous présente ma femme, dont vous connaissez déjà le patron.
5 C'est un livre sans lequel je ne comprendrais rien du tout!
6 Celui qui est riche est toujours populaire.
7 Ma robe est noire, mais je préfère celle qui est bleue.
8 Sa mère à lui est difficile, mais la mienne est charmante.
9 J'ai acheté le CD d'un excellent chanteur dont j'ai oublié le nom.
10 Ma valise est lourde, mais les siennes sont très légères.

Translate into French:

11 There are two flats. Which do you prefer?
12 Do you know the family whose son is a film director?
13 Which tart do you prefer? The apple or the chocolate?
14 That's my penfriend, to whom I write every month.
15 Look at the cars. Which do you like best?
16 Whose cats are those? Are they yours?
17 The one with the pretty pictures, that's the book I'd like.
18 They have several houses, but I prefer the one by the sea.
19 The blue handbag? That's mine!
20 That's the book I need!

A2 Grammar: more complex tenses

What you need to know

At A2 Level you are expected to be familiar with the use of the more complex tenses:

► the future perfect: *j'aurai fini* – I will have finished; *tu seras parti* – you will have left

► the conditional perfect: *j'aurais voulu* – I would have wanted; *nous aurions fait* – we should have done: *j'aurais dû le savoir* – I should have known that

► the passive voice in all tenses: *il sera fait* – it will be done; *ceci a été décidé* – this has been decided; *ils étaient transportés* – they were transported

You also need to be able to use dependent infinitives, such as *faire réparer. Vous le ferez réparer?* Will you have it repaired? *Je vous ferai voir.* I will show you.

(9) Translate into English:

1 Dans l'avenir, les choses auront beaucoup changé.
2 Par exemple, le gouvernement aura pris des mesures pour limiter les déplacements.
3 Les scientifiques auront développé des moyens de transport non-polluants.
4 On aura inventé beaucoup de nouvelles machines, qui nous rendront la vie quotidienne plus confortable.
5 Je n'aurais jamais cru que tout cela serait possible.
6 Vous auriez pu le deviner!
7 Oui, mais si on m'avait dit qu'il serait normal de prendre ses vacances sur la lune, j'aurais nié la possibilité.
8 Tout cela était expliqué par les scientifiques.
9 Mais est-ce que ce sera fait un jour?
10 Beaucoup de changements ont déjà été faits.

Translate into French:

11 It will never be done.
12 We will have seen the programme already.
13 Will you have bought the present?
14 They won't have visited Toulouse.
15 You would have liked Amiens.
16 But they would not have bought any souvenirs.
17 I should have said no.
18 He could have gone by car.
19 She had her bike repaired.
20 It was damaged in an accident.

Listening to plenty of French helps improve your pronunciation. So will working through specific exercises like the ones below. It can be tricky to correct bad habits, so if a teacher or assistant gives you advice on the way you pronounce a particular sound, make a written note of it and refer back to it occasionally to make sure you really have remembered it.

1 Les voyelles: a, è, é, i, o, u

Écoutez et répétez le son de six voyelles françaises.

a	habite, déjà, femme	a à e + mm
è	frère, fête, treize, aide, aîné vaisselle, ancienne princesse, baguette	è ê ei ai aî e + ll, e + nn, e + ss, e + tt
é	télévision, lycée, aller, pied, chez, mes effet, essayer	é ée er ed ez es e + ff, e + ss
i	ici, dîner, lycée, égoïste, prix, nuit	i î y ix it ï
o	chose, faux, beaucoup, bientôt	o au eau ô
u	musique, sûr	u û

2 Les sons 'é', 'ais', 'è', 'ère', 'er'

Écoutez et répétez ces différents sons français.

é – liberté, réussir, métier, école, indépendant
ai, ais – faire, aide, maison, parfait, vraiment
è – bibliothèque, système, succède, être, crêpes
ère – chère, père, mère, frère, colère
er – aller, donner, changer, essayer, expliquer

3 Les sons 'in', 'an', 'on', 'un', 'en'

Écoutez et répétez ces différents sons français.

in – intéressant, international, matin, important, impossible, pain, plein, peinture
an – vacances, océan, restaurant, pendant, blanc, chambre
on – rencontrer, dont, combien, nombreux, complet
un – un, chacun, brun, opportun
en – moment, enrichissant, alimentation, empêcher, temps

4 Les liaisons

Lisez ces phrases à haute voix en faisant attention aux liaisons. Écoutez pour vérifier.

1 De nombreux accidents de la route sont tout à fait évitables.
2 Il y a un écart de huit ans entre l'espérance de vie des hommes et des femmes.

3 À trois heures dix, six voitures entraient en collision sur l'autoroute du soleil.

4 À Paris, il y a parfois quatre ou cinq pharmacies les unes après les autres.

5 L'intonation: questions et exclamations

L'intonation: la voix monte ou descend. Écoutez et répétez.

1 Les questions simples: Tu vas au lycée? Aimez-vous votre lycée?
Les questions avec un interrogatif: À quel âge es-tu allé au lycée?
Que pensez-vous du lycée?
Les questions – énumération: Tu es pour ou contre? Tu envisages des études longues, des études courtes ou la vie active?
Les exclamations: Alors là, catastrophe! Moi, j'adore mon lycée!

Lisez tout haut, puis écoutez pour vérifier et répétez.

2 En quelle année es-tu entré en sixième? Tu es allé dans un lycée après?
Tu préfères les maths ou le français? Moi, je vais y arriver! Tu fais anglais, allemand ou italien? Je déteste ça!

6 Le 'r' français

En français, il faut rouler le 'r' un peu dans la gorge. Écoutez et répétez.

1 rouge, rhythme, rollers, repas, relax, racontez
2 Arrêtez! Je suis arrivé.
3 c'est fermé, moderne, le chef du personnel
4 j'ai travaillé, j'ai préparé, j'ai créé
5 Robert m'a raconté qu'elle avait regardé les répétitions.
6 Valérie rentre en France au printemps.

7 Les consonnes que l'on ne prononce pas

En général, les consonnes s, t, d, p, x placées à la fin d'un mot ne se prononcent pas. Écoutez et lisez, puis répétez.

1 s – accès excès Paris   s – les médias préférées des jeunes
t – le débat, le droit de tout savoir   d, x – Le Canard Enchaîné, La Voix
                                                           du Nord
p – Il y a beaucoup trop de publicité à la télé.

Cependant, des consonnes se prononcent lorsqu'elles sont suivies d'un 'e'. Écoutez et lisez, puis répétez.

2 les Français   la radio française   il est mort   elle est morte
il fait chaud   des températures chaudes

8 'o' ouvert – o fermé – ou

Écoutez et répétez les trois sons:

1 'o' ouvert – solaire, bénévole, solution
'o' fermé – beau, frigo, eau
'ou' – souvent, trouver, groupe

Classez ces mots en trois listes selon le son souligné, puis vérifiez en écoutant.

sauvage nocif pelouse douche oiseau toxique les Vosges nouvelle bloc-notes seau politique renouvelable

2 'o' ouvert – nocif, toxique, bloc-notes, politique

  'o' fermé – sauvage, oiseau, les Vosges, seau

  'ou' – pelouse, douche, nouvelle, renouvelable

Lisez les phrases à haute voix. Écoutez pour vérifier et répétez.

3 Tu es populaire avec tes co-équipiers? Il nous faut une nouvelle politique sur la technologie. L'opération de communication a été un grand succès. Les bénévoles espèrent sauver les oiseaux des produits toxiques.

9 Prononciation de 'in' et 'im'

in-/im- + consonne sauf n et m   im-/im- + voyelle, n, m

Écoutez et répétez.

intégration, interview, imbécile, important
inadmissible, innocent, image, immigré

10 L'accent de mot

L'accent principal du mot français tombe sur la dernière syllabe. Lisez les phrases. Écoutez pour vérifier et répétez.

C'est inexact de dire que l'immigration implique l'insécurité. L'inegalité des chances et l'injustice sont indéniables. Il est inacceptable et inexcusable qu'un pays industrialisé soit incapable d'intégrer des immigrés.

11 Les sons 'ille' et 'gn'

Écoutez et répétez.

1 ville, tranquille, mille, million, millier
2 fille, famille, billet, gentille, habillement
3 travailler, bouteille, accueille, ailleurs, j'aille, je veuille, grenouille, ratatouille
4 Allemagne, Espagne, Bretagne, Avignon, signer, ignore, oignon, enseignement
5 Des milliers de filles vivent à Avignon.
   On mange une bouillabaisse ou des cuisses de grenouille? Moi, je préfère de l'agneau avec une sauce à l'oignon. Des gentilles filles de la ville de Marseille font la ratatouille et la bouillabaisse à merveille.

12 Trois voyelles: 'a', 'u', 'o'

Écoutez et répétez.

1 Louisiane, Guyane, platane, banane
2 une, lune, dune, prune
3 couverture, voiture, écriture
4 francophone, anglophone, téléphone

Unit 1

l'effet de serre	the greenhouse effect
la révolution énergétique	the energy revolution
(réduire) nos besoins énergétiques	(to reduce) our energy needs
un panneau/capteur solaire	a solar panel
l'énergie solaire	solar energy
photovoltaïque	solar
innovateur	innovative
une éolienne	windmill/wind pump
une centrale (nucléaire)	(nuclear) power station
les déchets radioactifs	radioactive waste
la sécurité du nucléaire	nuclear safety
empêcher une catastrophe nucléaire	to prevent a nuclear catastrophe
une politique énergétique	an energy policy
la consommation d'énergie	energy consumption
la hausse des tarifs	the rise in prices
la recherche	research
s'épuiser	to run out
la déforestation	deforestation
le réchauffement climatique	global warming
polluer/polluant	to pollute/polluting
détruire/la destruction	to destroy/the destruction
disparaître/la disparition	to disappear/the disappearance
l'empreinte carbonique	carbon footprint
les produits pétroliers	oil products
dépendre du pétrole	to depend on oil
les stocks de charbon	stocks of coal
une interdiction	a ban
les gaz d'échappement (nocifs)	(toxic) exhaust fumes
les émissions	emissions
les avancées technologiques	technological advances
(éviter) le gaspillage	(to avoid) waste

Unit 2

les petits gestes (quotidiens)	small (everyday) gestures
être écolo	to be green
protéger/la protection	to protect/protection
sensibiliser/la sensibilisation	to make aware/awareness
une prise de conscience	awareness
réduire (l'impact de)/la réduction	to reduce (the impact of)/ reduction
agir/l'action	to act/action
sauvegarder la planète	to safeguard the planet
le développement durable	sustainable development

manifester/une manifestation	to demonstrate/ a demonstration
améliorer	to improve
changer le comportement	to change the behaviour
s'informer sur	to find out about
se servir de	to use
une exposition	an exhibition
un atelier (sur)	a workshop on
lutter contre/combattre	to fight against
des activistes	activists
éteindre les lumières	to put the lights out
baisser le chauffage	to turn the heating down
le co-voiturage	car-sharing
(trier) les déchets ménagers	(to separate) household rubbish
(utiliser) les bennes de recyclage	(to use) recycling bins
une ampoule basse consommation	a low energy lightbulb
recycler/le recyclage	to recycle/recycling
les pays industrialisés	industrialised countries
le bois coupé illégalement	illegally cut wood
à l'échelle mondiale	on a world scale

Unit 3

un immigré/l'immigration	immigrant/immigration
issu de l'immigration	immigrant (adj.)
(le statut de) réfugié	refugee (status)
un Français de souche/d'origine	born and bred Frenchman
le pays d'origine	country of origin
un étranger	a foreigner
s'installer/s'intégrer dans un pays	to settle/integrate in a country
le demandeur d'asile/le droit d'asile	asylum seeker/asylum
l'immigration clandestine	illegal immigration
les sans-papiers	illegal immigrants
obtenir la nationalité française	to obtain French nationality
le titre de séjour	residence permit
faire venir sa famille	to bring one's family over
se faire expulser/déporter	to be deported/to deport
être renvoyé	to be sent back
ouvrir les portes à tous	to open the doors to everyone
les origines/les racines	origins/roots
les pratiques culturelles	cultural practices
la peur de l'autre	the fear of others
l'inégalité des chances	inequality of opportunity
l'agitation sociale	social unrest
la discrimination (à l'embauche)	(employment) discrimination

le multiculturalisme	multiculturalism
la xénophobie	xenophobia, dislike of foreigners
être marginalisé	to be marginalised
imposer des quotas	to impose quotas
s'exacerber/s'améliorer	to get worse/to improve
un bouc émissaire	a scapegoat
les tensions raciales	racial tensions
la violence éclate	violence erupts
la banlieue	the suburb
les émeutes	riots
l'hostilité vis-à-vis de	hostility towards
se sentir étranger	to feel foreign
une association anti-raciste	anti-racist association
le respect mutuel	mutual respect
la tolérance/tolérer	tolerance/to tolerate
la double appartenance	belonging to two cultures
bilingue	bilingual

Unit 4

la misère/la pauvreté	poverty
les défavorisés/les plus démunis	the disadvantaged/most destitute
le seuil de pauvreté	the poverty threshold
les sans-abri	the homeless
sans logement	homeless (adj.)
les chômeurs/le chômage	the unemployed/unemployment
mendier/un mendiant	to beg/a beggar
le centre d'hébergement	hostel
le tiers-monde	the third world
les pays en voie de développement	developing countries
la malnutrition	malnutrition
les maladies infectieuses	infectious diseases
la guerre/la catastrophe	war/disaster
le tremblement de terre	earthquake
les soins médicaux/sanitaires	medical/health care
partager	to share
résoudre/affronter les problèmes	to solve/confront problems
favoriser la scolarisation	to encourage schooling
le commerce équitable	fair trade
vivre de son travail	to live from one's work
(lutter contre) l'exploitation	(to fight against) exploitation
le coton bio	organic cotton
une juste rémunération	fair pay
agir pour l'égalité	to work towards equality

Vocabulary

le micro-crédit	micro-credit
les petits prêts	small loans
(compter sur) la bonne volonté	(to count on) goodwill
les droits fondamentaux	basic rights
les valeurs éthiques	ethical values
verser une somme d'argent	to pay a sum of money
une œuvre/une association caritative	a charity
un magasin au profit d'une organisation caritative	a charity shop
une ONG (organisation non-gouvernementale)	a charity
soutenir/le soutien	to support/support
travailler comme bénévole	to work as a volunteer

Unit 5

l'agression (à main armée)	an (armed) attack
une bagarre	a fight, brawl
le cambriolage/un cambrioleur	burglary/a burglar
le trafic de drogues	drug trafficking
la dégradation de biens	damage to property
la fraude	fraud
le harcèlement sexuel	sexual harrassment
l'homicide involontaire	manslaughter
le meurtre/un meurtrier	murder/a murderer
le racket	extortion
le trafic de drogue	drug trafficking
l'usurpation d'identité	stealing someone's identity
le viol	rape
le vol/le voleur	theft/thief
la cybercriminalité	internet crime
les dégâts	damage
la délinquance juvénile/le délinquant	juvenile delinquency/delinquent
X euros de dommages	X euros worth of damage
la victime/l'accusé	the victim/the accused
un criminel (en herbe)	a (budding) criminal
arrêter	to arrest
le châtiment/punir	punishment/to punish
le procès	trial
coupable	guilty
accuser quelqu'un de ...	to accuse someone of ...
interpeller	to take in for questioning
récidiver	to re-offend
une amende	a fine
la prison/une peine de prison	prison/prison sentence

la réclusion à perpétuité	life imprisonment
être condamné à ...	to be sentenced to ...
six mois de prison (avec sursis)	six months of prison (suspended)
le bracelet électronique	electronic tag
la chambre correctionnelle des mineurs	youth justice court
(abolir) la peine de mort	(to abolish) the death penalty

Unit 6

la nouvelle technologie	new technology
les nouveaux horizons	new horizons
les OGM (organismes génétiquement modifiés)	GMOs
le clonage/cloner	cloning/to clone
la découverte/découvrir	discovery/to discover
le code (à) barres	bar code
programmer	to programme
numérique	digital
inventer/une invention	to invent/an invention
la société de surveillance	the surveillance society
limiter les déplacements	to limit journeys
faire ses achats au cybermarché/ sur Internet	to shop on the internet
voyager dans le temps	to travel in time
rendre la vie plus confortable	to make life more comfortable
la mise au point de	the development of
les parents porteurs d'un problème génétique	parents who carry a defective gene
une malformation congénitale	a congenital disorder
les maladies héréditaires	hereditary illnesses
guérir/la guérison	to cure/cure
les avancées génétiques	genetic advances
un problème éthique	an ethical problem
la greffe	transplant
le bébé-éprouvette	test-tube baby
le séquençage du génome humain	human gene sequencing
la recherche bio-médicale	biomedical research
l'ADN humain	human DNA
manipuler génétiquement	to manipulate genetically
diminuer l'utilisation des pesticides	to reduce the use of pesticides
association de protection des consommateurs	consumer protection society
du point du vue sanitaire	from a health point of view
tirer des bénéfices	to gain advantages
créer une banque d'organes	to create an organ bank

Unit 7

une œuvre	a work (of art)
la beauté/la vérité	beauty/truth
le goût	taste
le peintre/peindre	painter/to paint
dépeindre	to depict
le tableau/la toile	picture/painting
le paysage/le portrait	landscape/portrait
la lumière	light
les couleurs claires/sombres	light/dark colours
exposer/une exposition	to exhibit/an exhibition
un vif intérêt pour	a keen interest in
évoquer (une atmosphère)	to evoke (an atmosphere)
l'écrivain/l'auteur	writer/author
le romancier/le roman	novelist/novel
le caractère	personality
le personnage	character
le lecteur	the reader
un être imaginaire	imaginary being
raconter une histoire	to tell a story
traduit dans ... langues	translated into ... languages
une pièce de théâtre	a play
la scène	the stage
une comédie (de mœurs)	a comedy (of manners)
faire apparition à la télévision	to appear on television
un cinéaste/un réalisateur/un critique	a film-maker/director/critic
un film de long métrage	a full length film
la Nouvelle Vague	the New Wave
un César	French equivalent of an Oscar
interpréter un rôle	to play a role
l'action se déroule ...	the action takes place ...
tourner un film	to make a film
l'éclairage/le son	lighting/sound
le septième art	cinema
le spectateur	viewer
une renommée internationale	international fame
l'artisan	craftsman
le poète/la poésie	poet/poetry

Unit 8

francophone	French-speaking
les liens	links
la langue officielle/maternelle	official language/mother tongue

partager une langue	to share a language
une vague de colonisation	a wave of colonisation
des pays répartis sur cinq continents	countries spread over five continents
exercer une influence	to exert an influence
échapper à la pauvreté	to escape poverty
un atout important	a big advantage
à travers le monde	throughout the world
le conflit militaire	military conflict
le droit de s'exprimer	the right of expression
la censure	censorship
des mesures restrictives	restrictive measures
maintenir une influence	to have an influence
au niveau international	at an international level
les réalisations de l'UE	the achievements of the EU
faire face à la mondialisation	to cope with globalisation
harmoniser les politiques sur ...	to harmonise policies on ...
la liberté d'expression	freedom of expression
le patrimoine	heritage
essentiel à la survie économique	essential to economic survival
des dépenses inconsidérées	thoughtless expenditure
un député européen	an MEP
l'agrandissement	enlargement
appartenir à une réligion	to belong to a religion
être croyant/avoir la foi	to have faith
la croyance	belief
chrétien/musulman/juif	christian/muslim/jewish
l'esprit d'échange	the spirit of exchange
co-opérer/la co-opération	to co-operate/co-operation
être en déclin	to be in decline
baisser	to lower

Unit 9

faire entendre sa voix	to make one's voice heard
exprimer son opinion (sur)	to express one's opinion (on)
se présenter comme candidat	to stand as a candidate
le discours politique	political debate
le comité/le sous-comité	committee/sub-committee
les 35 heures	the 35 hour week
lancer une campagne	to launch a campaign
protester contre	to protest against
un communiqué de presse	a press release
une lettre à la rédaction	a letter to the editor
prononcer un discours	to deliver a speech

être préoccupé par	to be preoccupied by
se sentir concerné par	to feel concerned about/ affected by
l'Assemblée Nationale	the French Parliament
le Sénat	French Upper Chamber
un député	an MP
le ministre	minister
le ministère	ministry
le Conseil des Ministres	the cabinet
le premier ministre	the prime minister
un projet de loi	a (parliamentary) bill
se réunir	to meet
la circonscription	a constituency
une loi	a law
la politique étrangère	foreign policy
le Conseil Européen	the Council of Europe
le traité	treaty
la guerre (civile)	(civil) war
la tension/le conflit	tension/conflict
le sommet	summit meeting
renforcer sa présence militaire	to increase one's military presence
une campagne électorale/présidentielle	electoral/presidential campaign
fai re la guerre contre	to wage war against
s'allier avec	to ally oneself with
lutter contre le terrorisme	to fight terrorism
influencer l'opinion publique	to influence public opinion
une attaque chimique/nucléaire	a chemical/nuclear attack
sécuriser	to keep/make safe

1

1 We must use water which is less hot in the washing machine.
2 We see forest exploitation which is hardly respectful of nature.
3 We expect better next time!
4 Carbon gases have the worst effect on our atmosphere.
5 We have no more realistic solutions.
6 What should we do to take the right road?
7 The transport of the future will be much more efficient.
8 A varied diet is better for health.
9 I am clearly more optimistic than you are.
10 The sun brings us a direct source of light and heat.
11 Les trains sont moins polluants que les voitures.
12 Nous avons du gaz mais pas d'essence.
13 Une vieille voiture n'est pas bonne pour l'environnement.
14 Une nouvelle voiture est toute aussi mauvaise qu'une vieille.
15 Leur maison a des panneaux solaires.
16 Mon chauffage central est cher.
17 Il y a une bonne ambiance dans le village éco.
18 La vie là-bas est moins chère qu'ici.
19 Vous recyclez (Tu recycles) les journaux et les bouteilles?
20 Quelle énergie est la moins chère?

2

1 Immigrants? Do we pay them family allowance?
2 The latest immigration laws – do you know them?
3 The families of immigrants settled in the suburbs.
4 Xenophobia: who are its victims?
5 We all have the right to the nationality of the country in which we are born.
6 Immigrants came to work in our country. Are they happy here?
7 We are against measures which don't respect human rights.
8 France is the country where I grew up and whose culture I have completely absorbed.
9 People don't let me forget my Arab origins.
10 Respect? We do not always give it to them.
11 Explique(z)-moi le racisme.
12 Je leur ai dit que je ne le comprends pas.
13 Il habite le Sénégal et il y est très heureux.
14 C'est un pays que je ne connais pas.
15 Tahiti est un pays dont le climat est très agréable.
16 Ce sont des Polynésiens qui habitent la France.
17 Ils y habitent depuis vingt ans.
18 La carte? Montre(z)-la moi, s'il te (vous) plaît.
19 La xénophobie – quelle en est la cause?
20 Il faut la remplacer par la tolérance.

3

1 Do you prefer organising campaigns or working as a volunteer?
2 With their profits they support community projects.
3 Getting fair prices allows the producers to support their families.
4 We have to act to create fairer conditions.
5 Micro-credit has also been developing in the northern countries for about 10 years.

6 We are counting on the goodwill of all those who live in countries which are at peace.
7 We try to help these children find the joy of living again.
8 The pictures which are transmitted from the third world are often horrifying.
9 We must do all we can to help the victims of the earthquake.
10 Think about their problems before judging them.
11 Cela garantit un certain niveau de vie.
12 Tu travailles (Vous travaillez) pour une organisation caritative?
13 Je veux aider les gens à mener une vie indépendante.
14 On ne peut pas compter sur la bonne volonté des gens!
15 J'espère pouvoir aider.
16 Qu'est-ce que tu as (vous avez) décidé de faire?
17 Il organise des campagnes depuis des années.
18 Ils font tout ce qu'ils peuvent pour construire une maison.
19 Dépenser tout son argent, c'est ridicule!
20 Que font les gens s'ils ne peuvent pas trouver un emploi?

1 The poet Charles Baudelaire was tried for immorality.
2 In 1919 the expression *Le septième art* was suggested to describe cinematography.
3 It was a time when society was dominated by men.
4 As soon as he had left school, François Truffaut founded a cinema club.
5 For Camus, God didn't exist and so you had to make the most of your life.
6 Godard, Truffaut and Chabrol set about making different films.
7 Truffaut always wanted to take his inspiration from his own life.
8 In *Les quatre cent coups*, the young actor addressed the camera directly.
9 Yasmina Reza grew up in a cultural environment. She hoped to become a sociologist.
10 Having studied theatre, Yasmina Reza began to work as an actress.
11 Combien de personnes ont visité le Musée d'Orsay en 2007?
12 Cette peinture a été vendue pour $78,000,000 l'année dernière.
13 Albert Camus est devenu journaliste en 1938.
14 Dans ses romans, il décrivait toujours les gens et les situations de tous les jours.
15 Berthe Morisot a été choquée par l'exposition de 1874.
16 Truffaut voulait toujours tourner des films réalistes.
17 Il a gagné un César et un Oscar.
18 Yasmina Reza a-t-elle écrit de la poésie?
19 Ayant été actrice, elle a commencé à écrire des pièces de théâtre.
20 Jusqu'à hier, je n'avais vu aucune de ses pièces.

1 Tomorrow we will live in a world guided by computers.
2 In the future, computers will help you choose everything.
3 It will be practically unnecessary to leave the house.
4 Scientists' decisions will have serious consequences.
5 We will have the possibility of curing many hereditary illnesses.
6 But there will be no miracle cure in the next five years.
7 Any genetic pollution would be irreversible.
8 Genetic manipulation could create a world where the people are too perfect.
9 All meat should have a label which tells you where it has come from.
10 If you asked my opinion, I wouldn't know what to say.
11 Comment vivrons-nous dans l'avenir?

12 Il y aura des ordinateurs partout.
13 Nous ferons nos achats au cybermarché.
14 Tu pourras (Vous pourrez) passer tes (vos) vacances sur une autre planète.
15 Comment sera la vie de tous les jours?
16 Mon ordinateur m'aidera à prendre des décisions.
17 Les scientifiques devront être très responsables.
18 Je ne voudrais pas vivre dans un monde parfait.
19 Les gens devraient en savoir plus sur la technologie.
20 Quand tu seras (vous serez) vieux (vieille) tu auras (vous aurez) besoin des ordinateurs.

1 Let's not forget the importance of cultural diversity.
2 Don't be afraid of the European Union!
3 For the moment, the EU has neither a president nor an army.
4 It has never been a question of saying no.
5 Even those who fear losing their identity cannot deny the advantages of the EU.
6 Here we will mention only a few projects such as the Airbus and the Ariane rocket.
7 Nor is the EU short of ideas for the future.
8 This is especially true of people who are not French nationals.
9 Shouldn't the Irish have said 'yes' to the Treaty of Lisbon?
10 Perhaps they prefer no longer to be a member of the EU.
11 La Pologne n'est-elle pas membre de l'UE?
12 Il n'avait pas voté.
13 Tu ne visiteras (Vous ne visiterez) jamais la Russie.
14 L'UE n'a que 27 états membres.
15 Je n'aimerais pas être Président de l'UE!
16 Je n'ai plus de passeport.
17 Rien n'est plus certain.
18 Il ne me reste aucun euro.
19 Tu préfères (Vous préférez) ne pas prendre tes (vos) vacances en France?
20 Je n'ai ni le temps ni l'argent.

1 We moved so that I can go to a good lycée.
2 Providing I pass the bac, I will study at university.
3 Although they are not well paid, they like their work.
4 Whatever you do in France, you have to know how to speak French.
5 I doubt that we can change things quickly.
6 I want to fit in in France, but I don't believe that means I have to forget my origins.
7 It's not certain that I am well integrated.
8 I do not want the National Front to get into power.
9 I don't regret that my parents always talked to me in Arabic.
10 Ali is ashamed that his mother has never learned to speak French.
11 J'irai à condition que tu viennes (vous veniez) avec moi.
12 Moi, je suis contente qu'elle soit loin.
13 Il a déménagé à Paris afin que ses enfants puissent apprendre le français.
14 Il n'est pas certain qu'elle ait raison.
15 Il faut que nous allions voir.
16 Nous devrons faire des recherches avant que tu choisisses (vous choisissiez) une université.

17 Ce sera bien pourvu qu'il fasse beau.
18 C'est la plus grande glace que j'aie jamais vue.
19 Je veux partir avant qu'il rentre.
20 Qu'il soit riche ou non, je l'aime.

1   The beautiful girls? Which ones?
2   And the 100 Euro notes. Are they yours?
3   He is a man to whom I owe everything.
4   This is my wife, whose boss you already know.
5   It is a book without which I would understand nothing at all.
6   He who is rich is always popular.
7   My dress is black, but I prefer the blue one.
8   His mother is difficult, but mine is charming.
9   I bought a CD by an excellent singer whose name I have forgotten.
10 My case is heavy, but his (hers) are very light.
11 Il y a deux appartements. Lequel préfères-tu (préférez-vous)?
12 Tu connais (Vous connaissez) la famille dont le fils est metteur en scène?
13 Tu préfères (Vous préférez) quelle tarte? Celle aux pommes ou celle au chocolat?
14 Voilà le correspondant (la correspondante) auquel (à laquelle) j'écris tous les mois.
15 Regarde (Regardez) les voitures. Laquelle préfères-tu (préférez-vous)?
16 À qui sont ces chats? Ce sont les tiens (les vôtres)?
17 Celui aux belles images, voilà le livre dont j'ai envie.
18 Ils ont plusieurs maisons, mais moi je préfère celle au bord de la mer.
19 Le sac à main bleu? C'est le mien!
20 Voilà le livre dont j'ai besoin.

1   In the future, things will have changed a great deal.
2   For example, the government will have taken measures to limit journeys.
3   Scientists will have developed non-polluting means of transport.
4   We will have invented lots of new machines which will have made daily life more comfortable.
5   I would never have thought all that would be possible.
6   You could have guessed.
7   Yes, but if you had told me it would be normal to holiday on the moon, I would have denied that it was possible.
8   All this was explained by scientists.
9   But will this be done one day?
10 Lots of changes have already been made.
11 Ça ne se fera jamais.
12 Nous aurons déjà vu l'émission.
13 Est-ce que tu auras (Vous aurez) déjà acheté le cadeau?
14 Ils n'auront pas visité Toulouse.
15 Tu aurais (Vous auriez) aimé Amiens.
16 Mais ils n'auraient pas acheté de souvenirs.
17 J'aurais dû dire non.
18 Il aurait pu y aller en voiture.
19 Elle a fait réparer son vélo.
20 Il a été abîmé dans un accident.